# Made for More

## A 6-Week Journey

# Made for More

## A 6-Week Journey

### By Deanna Doss Shrodes

Entourage Publishing

Entourage Publishing
Ann Arbor, MI

*Made for More,
A 6-Week Journey*
By Deanna Doss Shrodes

Copyright 2020 Deanna Doss Shrodes.
All rights reserved.

License Notes
This book is licensed for your personal enjoyment only. This book may not be re-sold or given away to other people. If you would like to share it with another person, please purchase an additional copy for each recipient. If you're reading this book and did not purchase it, or it was not purchased for your use only, then please return to Amazon.com and purchase your own copy. Thank you for respecting the hard work of the author.

Entourage Publishing, 2020
Paperback ISBN: 978-1-942312-13-0

Editor: Laura Dennis

Cover Art by Linda Boulanger (2020)
Tell-Tale Book Cover Designs

# Dedication

*I dedicate this book to my daughter, Savanna Rose.*

*Your name means, "peaceful gift from God," and indeed you are such a gift from God.*

*I love you,*
*Mom*

# Contents

Preface ..................................................................2
Chapter 1 — You Were Made for More Than Rules ........5
Chapter 2 — You Were Made for More Than Toxic Thoughts ....................................................................15
Chapter 3 — You Were Made for More Than Unhealthy Relationships ..................................................27
Chapter 4 — You Were Made for More Than Secrets ...41
Chapter 5 — You Were Made for More Than Shrinking 57
Chapter 6 — You Were Made for More than Exhaustion ............................................................................75
Want More from Deanna? ...........................................86
Acknowledgements ......................................................87
About the Author .........................................................89
References ...................................................................91

# Made for More

## A 6-Week Journey

# Preface

In the Spring of 2020, Covid-19 affected the entire world, locking countries and communities down into isolation. It became clear that I was going to be working from home for weeks, maybe months, on end. This meant a temporary end to my two-hour-a-day commute. PF Women, the ministry that I lead, had to cancel our leadership conference, followed by many other seemingly endless cancellations. All the while, we were getting reports of the death toll daily around the world. Like millions of other people, I was facing disappointment and uncertainty.

During those days, my assistant, Judi, and I began to plan the restructuring of our summer tour for the year, the theme of which was, "Made for More." This is our biggest event for women every year, reaching several thousand women all over the state of Florida.

One thing that was still allowed in our community during lockdown was outdoor exercise, by oneself. I began daily walks of about three miles. During those times, I would think, pray, and ask God to help me make lemonade out of lemons.

As I walked one day, God clearly spoke to me, "In the next month you are to write a book entitled *Made for More* that will be a 6-week journey for women. Write it in April, publish it in May and have it ready to give to every woman on the upcoming tour starting June 1."

I knew this would require writing a book in a month, but what God ordains will succeed.

While *Made for More* was written for the women of the Pen Florida District of the Assemblies of God, I believe it will encourage many other women for the glory of God.

While you can read straight through the book (I confess—I always do that, even when it's a chapter-a-week study), I recommend that you come back and focus on one topic per week. This will give you some time to work on each of these important issues in your life and start to make steps forward.

No matter what has happened in your life, be assured you are made for more than you realize. You are also made for more than others acknowledge. What you are made for will astound you if you ever comprehend the totality of it!

# Chapter 1 — You Were Made for More Than Rules

*Legalism says God will love us if we change. The gospel says God will change us because He loves us.*
*~ Tullian Tchividjian*

No one was home. It was eerily silent.

A flash of fear washed over me.

Grandma Lewis took care of me before and after school during my younger years. She was the best. Not only was she the best Grandma ever, she was also the Godliest as far as I was concerned. That day, she wasn't there when I came home.

When she didn't answer after I called out to her to let her know I was home, I immediately become concerned. I darted through the house, to the back porch and into the yard, even searching behind Grandpa's tool shed. My heart seemed to pound out of my chest. My thought was, "I didn't make it." It seemed like the room was spinning around as I became filled with anxiety.

# 6

I was convinced the rapture had taken place, and I was left behind.

I started weeping and continued to do so, until Grandma came home from the neighbor's house where she had been helping someone. I was relieved; all was still well. As I grew older, and she was not watching me before or after school, if I believed I had been left behind, I dialed her phone number. As soon as I heard her voice, I knew I was alright. Grandma would have never been left behind. If she was still there, everyone was okay, at least for the moment.

I'm grateful for my Christian heritage. There were upsides and downsides to my personal spiritual formation. The positives were that I was taught gobs of the Bible. My mother worked with me on memorizing several chapters of the Bible when I was barely a toddler. At just a few years old I could recite Psalm 100 and Psalm 23. I grew up on sword drills. Our church emphasized the Holy Spirit. We heard a lot about heaven and hell. I'm so thankful – because it's real! Most of what I learned about the Bible I learned as a kid. At the same time, a missing piece in my spiritual formation was hearing enough about how much God loved me and wanted to spend time with me. I learned this on my own, many years later.

My favorite book that I use in spiritually mentoring people is *Secrets of the Secret Place* by Bob Sorge. It was through this book that I learned so many things I lacked earlier on in my spiritual journey. One of the things that meant the most to me that I discovered is that when I fail to spend time with God, He's not mad at me. He's sad for me. The reason He is sad is because He loves me, wants to spend time with me, and has so much for me. It took me decades to understand God this way.

I made some of the biggest mistakes of my life before I understood his love. I discovered that when you understand how much God loves you, your behavior changes. That's because your heart changes. Although I take joy in following God's commands, my relationship with Him now is not based on a fear of missing the rapture. My walk with Him is rooted and grounded in His love. I know He loves me, accepts me, forgives me, and that is what keeps me tethered to Him, longing to spend time with Him.

There are some unbelievable rules that exist today.

**Did you know…**

- In Hawaii, it's illegal to put a coin in your ear.[1] (I don't advise trying this.)

- In Indiana, it's illegal to ride a horse over 10 miles per hour.[2] (Make sure you install a speedometer on your horse…)

- In Maine, it's illegal to park in front of Dunkin Donuts.[3] (I'd be in trouble if I lived in Maine.)

There were astonishing rules in the Bible, too. Before Jesus came to earth as a human being, died on the cross for our sins and was resurrected, the number of rules people had to follow were astronomical. It was impossible to obey all of them, even if that was all they focused on. Sacrifices were continually required in order to be forgiven for sins. Then Jesus made the ultimate sacrifice once and for all…for us, so that all of humankind could be forgiven and have eternal life.

**You were made for more than rules.**

**You were made for love.**

Zephaniah 3:17 (NIV) says, "The Lord your God is with you, the Mighty Warrior who saves. He will take great delight in you; in His love He will no longer rebuke you but will rejoice over you with singing."

God sings over you. Rejoices over you. He takes such delight in you. God does not just tolerate you. The love He has for you bubbles up so much within Him that He sings over you and takes delight in you.

The reason people don't surrender to God is because they haven't understood the depth of His love and care for them.

"They don't surrender because they want their own way…" some will say.

Perhaps, but consider that they only want their own way because they haven't unearthed the truth, that whatever God has for them blows whatever they envisioned for themselves out of the water!

We will always accept second best for our lives when we are not living in an understanding of God's unconditional, everlasting love for us. Will we totally understand it this side of heaven? No. But God reveals so much to us when we open ourselves up to receive His love.

This is one of the reasons the enemy tries so hard to give people any image of God other than One who delights in them. If he can just convince people of another type of God, he's got them in a trap. Bob Sorge says, "Nothing is deadlier to the secret place than a false idea of how God views you; and nothing is more powerfully energizing than when your mind is renewed in the Word of God and you come to understand how He looks on you."[4]

Perhaps this is also why Jesus reserved some of His strongest words for those who were legalistic!

Legalism is when we excessively adhere to laws or rules rather than depending on the grace and mercy of God. The Pharisees were the most religious people during the time Jesus walked the earth. In scripture we can see they were the ones who developed a comprehensive list of rules to keep from breaking the law. And yet, they gave Jesus the most trouble! They didn't understand who God really is. For them, He was simply a rule maker, not one to be in close relationship with. They failed to grasp that it was all about the heart, not rules. In response to their behavior, Jesus condemned the Pharisees and even pronounced seven woes upon them!

When we become legalistic, our focus is totally off. We become all about behavior modification and not heart change. We can have all the right outward behaviors but still not know God at all.

Early on in my journey of serving as District Women's Director, someone asked why I was not taking a public stand against women wearing yoga pants. Well, first I'd have to stop wearing *my* yoga pants. [Full disclosure: I've never been to a yoga class. I just love the pants! So comfy!] Majoring in these types of minor issues doesn't move anyone closer to Christ. It causes needless debate and distraction. When I take a public stand on something, I want it to be about, "For God so loved the world..." not a pair of yoga pants.

One of the amazing things about Jesus is that when we surrender to Him and He changes our heart, the adhering to the mandates of His word seems to almost take care of itself. It is within our close walk with the Holy Spirit that the boundaries are laid out by Him concerning where we go, what we do, what we wear, and so forth.

No one ever changes because of rules, but plenty of people change because of love.

People try so hard to change and many never actually do. Why? Because it's all based on their own effort and not God's power.

Instead of trying harder, we must surrender more.

When you know you are loved, you behave differently.

## Marisela Santiago's Story

I was always looking to fit in. I searched for acceptance, trying to prove to others that I was able to get things done and get credit for it. I was overlooked, in my younger years, and always disappointed. Most of the time I wanted the approval of my parents or for them to say words like, "Wow! You are doing a great job," or "I'm proud of you." But this never happened. This continued well into adulthood, and I was always seeking reassurance from someone. I came to know the Lord in my early adult years, but I still carried an intense need for acceptance.

One day, I was watching a Christian woman on television and she said, "You can ask God to let you see what you need to be accepted and have assurance. He will show you." So, I asked God, and He said to me "When you see what you are worth to me, and the value that you are to me, you will understand what you are worth. I need you. You are my masterpiece." Something shifted inside of me and as I looked myself in the mirror, I stared to speak to myself about what God said to me. I said, "I am a masterpiece."

God reassured me of His love, and my heart surrendered and was open to receive and accept His love for me. Then I came to see that what God has for me is greater than anything else in the world. That was the day everything changed in my life. I felt that I could do and accomplish tasks without the need for someone else's reassurance, even though it's always nice to hear it. It is amazing what has taken place in my life once I accepted God's love for me![5]

My friend, what would happen in your life if you completely surrendered to the love of God?

**This Week's Assignments:**

- Check out the Christian artist, Julie True. Get her music on Spotify, iTunes or wherever you listen to music. (You can listen to some of her music for free on YouTube.) Get alone in a quiet room. Lie down with a pillow or two and get comfortable. Play some of Julie's music, and just listen. Don't speak, don't sing, don't ask Him for anything, just let God love you. Maybe you have never allowed yourself to just be still and feel the love of God. This is your week!

- Several times during the day, breathe this one sentence prayer: "God, I receive your love..." Do this especially when you feel unloved, unsettled, or lonely.

- Write down the loving words God speaks to you, for you. Write back to Him.

- Post on social media about what God is showing you this week. Use the hashtags #PFWMadeforMore #Morethanrules

**On This Week's Playlist:**

Everything Julie True has ever recorded, *Reckless Love* by Cory Asbury, and *Good, Good Father* by Chris Tomlin

# Chapter 2 — You Were Made for More Than Toxic Thoughts

*I've had enough of hustling for my worth. I've had enough of groveling to people unworthy of me for scraps of love or time or attention. I've had enough of keeping people in my life who diminish me. And I've had enough of trying to be anything other than me... because I, in all my imperfect, messy glory, am perfectly ENOUGH.*
*~ Mandy Hale, You Are Enough*

What you think is extremely important. Ralph Waldo Emerson once said, "Life consists of what a man is thinking about all day."

Believing everything you think is dangerous. You can talk yourself out of anything because of faulty thinking. In fact, you will talk yourself right out of every good thing destined to happen for you!

Many women believe they are incapable...that they are not enough. This false belief has been reinforced over time as people in their life tell them they don't have what it takes.

If you've been told you aren't enough, you're not alone.

Oprah Winfrey was an evening news reporter and was told by producers that she was unsuitable because she couldn't sever her emotions from her stories. Eventually she was fired by the producer of Baltimore's WJZ-TV.[6]

Before she starred on the TV show, *I Love Lucy*, Lucille Ball was considered a failed actress. Her drama instructors urged her to try another profession.[7]

Meryl Streep once dealt with a film director who insulted her looks and asked why she had even bothered to show up for the audition.[8]

Before starring in *My Big Fat Greek Wedding,* Nia Vardalos was initially told that that there were simply no roles for Greek American actresses, and she would never get to represent her background on screen.[9]

J.K. Rowling was rejected by twelve publishers before making it big, and was told, "Don't quit your day job!"[10]

Marilyn Monroe was told, "You should be a secretary, not a model."[11]

You are not the first woman who has been told she's not enough and doesn't have what it takes, and, unfortunately, you won't be the last.

**Dianna Walston's Story**

I was adopted into a Christian home. They loved me as best they could. However, many of my adoptive family members were not happy about me being part of the family. There was a huge age difference between my siblings and myself. All I wanted was to be loved and to be accepted. I was teased and continually put down. I worked for approval in every part of my life. I had numerous unhealthy friendships and I felt very alone. I had gone to the altar many times and begged God to heal me and to help me, to love me. I wanted to be free of this burden of feeling unloved, unwanted and unworthy. I often became a doormat in a variety of relationships and would be filled with resentment because of feeling used. My precious husband tried to help me but was unable to fill my need for acceptance. I truly believed that even God had forgotten about me. Just three years ago God finally got through to my head and my heart. He placed incredible Godly people in my life that prayed with and for me. I was finally able to understand that I was loved, accepted and a precious child of the King. I am spending time in God's Word and I finally gave my burdens to Him completely. I have learned the importance of taking a Sabbath and taking care of me so that I am then able to help others. I am free and I am whole. I lead worship and feel so free to praise Him with no reservation. I am worthy and I am enough. Only God can fill that true need and once I realized that HE was my answer everything else has fallen into place.

More than likely, all of us have had the experience of being diminished or used by someone in our lives. Some women have been outright oppressed or abused.

Leadership expert John Maxwell says:

Those who develop the process of good thinking can rule themselves – even while under an oppressive ruler or in other difficult circumstances. I've studied successful people for forty years and although the diversity you find among them is astounding, I've found that they are alike in one way – how they think![12]

So how do we make sure we are thinking the right way?

The first thing to realize is that we don't think the right way by accident. Keeping our thoughts on the right course is something that must be done intentionally. To fail to do so can have dire consequences.

Dr. Caroline Leaf is well known for her studies on the brain and thinking. Since the early 1980s she has researched the mind-brain connection, the nature of mental health, and the formation of memory. Leaf says:

If you let your toxic emotions grow unchecked by constantly thinking about them and ruminating on your feelings, you will feel worse because the resultant neurochemical chaos will cause brain damage and dramatically affect your mental and physical wellbeing. Do you really want to give people that much power over your life? Remember, if words control you, then everyone can control you![13]

We need to surrender control to the Holy Spirit. In order to do this, everything that goes through our minds needs to be filtered through the Word of God Romans 12:2 tells us that we need to be transformed by the renewal of our minds so that by testing, we can discern the will of God and what is acceptable and perfect.

Who decides what is acceptable? Who deems something perfect?

## Pamela Clayton's Story

As a child, my siblings and I suffered a lot. Unfortunately, we did not have a stable home and everything we did was under scrutiny. I never felt that I was good enough or that I even mattered to anyone because of the lack of love in my home. This created in me a sense of feeling that nothing I did was worth anything and that my voice did not need to be heard, as I had nothing worth speaking. I felt like God couldn't use me because I was too weak-minded, and I could not stand before anyone. When I became a Christian I still struggled because I still felt this way. If anyone exhibited any behavior resembling what I experienced as a child, I would clam up. Then, God showed me what was happening. I discovered that I was relating to Him as I had been relating to people. It broke something in me, and I began to see myself as He did. I realized that I was not what was done to me. It freed me to be me. I still struggle at times. But God reassures me in those times that I am who He made me to be and that He is pleased. So when I feel like I'm not enough, or maybe someone else should do a task that I have been asked to do, or fill a role that I have been asked to fill, He gently reminds me, "It is you I want."[14]

Like Pamela, we must remind ourselves constantly of what God says about us.

The question is, what does God think? What does God say? What is God speaking to you?

In his book, *Whisper: How to Hear the Voice of God*, Mark Batterson asks the question, "Is God's voice the loudest voice in your life?"[15]

If God's voice is not the loudest voice in your life, you will miss out, big time.

You will miss out on relationships, opportunities, interactions, great times of joy – and God's will in general. To follow God's will, we must hear His voice.

The enemy will tell you all the reasons you are disqualified, and, sadly, many people will harmonize with him in singing that song to you. And then, there are people who will refuse to chime in with him and will speak His truth to you. Terry Raburn was and is one such person for me.

When I was first considering furthering my education, I didn't pursue it, mainly because I convinced myself I couldn't pass a math class. I always saw myself as "less than" academically. I thought all majors probably required at least one math class. Although I excelled in my other classes as I was growing up, I could barely make a passing grade in mathematics and sometimes I failed. I have many memories of sitting at the kitchen table with tears streaming down my face as I did my math homework. Concepts like multiplication and division would be explained to me repeatedly and the person might as well have been speaking Greek. I was tutored for years, and still didn't improve. Adults would get frustrated with me many times and claim I wasn't listening, or really trying. Over and over I would hear,

"You just need to apply yourself." I didn't know what more I could do to apply myself. As a teen, although I was willing to work any job, I avoided ones like being a store cashier where you had to make change. I couldn't do it quickly and would give people the wrong change. Many times, throughout adulthood, I have been embarrassed at the lack of ability to do math problems in my head and my IQ score reduced me to tears. Any IQ test I ever took was mostly arithmetic-related.

I didn't know until I was in my late thirties that I had a learning disorder. This was discovered by accident. After suffering headaches for months, I was referred to a specialist who thoroughly checked my head, neck and brain. I underwent all sorts of tests, including an MRI and a written test where I had to do things like recite the alphabet and numbers forward and backwards and draw a picture of the United States, as well as other shapes. As the doctor was speaking to his assistant, who was recording everything in my chart, he turned to her and said, "This patient suffers from mathematical dyslexia." I was absolutely stunned to realize this had been my problem growing up, and it was never identified. Somehow, I had made it successfully to adulthood, barely knowing that two plus two equals four. (Thank you, calculators!) Suddenly, everything made sense.

When I was presented with the opportunity of being District Women's Director, I realized I had this learning disorder, but I also felt God wanted me to accept the position. I also knew the department was in a lot of debt and would need someone with the wisdom to fix that situation. Although I didn't know math, and even balancing a checkbook took me more time than it did most people, I knew leadership. I've always felt money problems are a result of bad stewardship, not bad mathematics. So, I accepted the job, knowing that I could work on the budget at my own pace and have help from others, such as those who worked in the finance department. I thanked God repeatedly for folks like Jane Grinstead, who was CFO when I arrived, and now Greg Rodden, our current CFO, who were, and still are, so patient with me. Not only did we get out of the debt we were in, but the finances increased by 195% over my first five years in office. Not bad for a mathematical dyslexic!

When my boss, Terry Raburn, spoke to me about going back to school for my master's, I hung my head in shame and said, "I don't think I can pass whatever math classes would be necessary." He said, "There are no math classes at the master's level for this major." I could hardly believe my ears, and was even more shocked when, with tears in his eyes he said, " believe one day I will be sitting across from Dr. Deanna Shrodes." I told him he was crazy. I didn't think I could do the master's, let alone a doctorate. He was undaunted and believed in me and supported me going back to school.

This is not to brag on me but to brag on God, and to encourage every other woman out there. The last time I was in school, computers did not exist, libraries online did not exist, online classes did not exist. This was a whole new world that, quite frankly, scared me a little bit. Nevertheless, I enrolled. I graduated with a master's degree, carrying a 3.91 grade point average. As of this writing, I am a doctoral student, scheduled to graduate in May of 2022!

If I can do all this as a person who can barely add and subtract, what can you do?

You may think you can't do it, but if God says you can, you can!

You may think you aren't qualified, but God is the one who qualifies!

You may think you don't measure up, but it's God who sets the standard!

You may think you aren't enough, but God says YOU ARE ENOUGH!

We do not have control over every thought that crosses our mind, but we do have control over whether to continue with that thought or dwell on it. As someone once said, "You may be given a cactus, but you don't have to sit on it!"

You can dwell on what you don't have, or you can focus on what you do have.

You can also focus on what the Terry Raburns of your life say rather than what the naysayers say!

2 Corinthians 10:5 tells us that we need to destroy arguments and every opinion raised against the knowledge of God and take every thought captive to Christ.

To take something captive is to imprison it, confine it and control it. If you take a thought captive, you seize it and force it to go where you want it to go. You imprison the thought – confine it and control it.

The truth is –

You are capable.

You are called.

You are anointed.

You do have what it takes.

You can do this.

You are enough.

**This Week's Assignments:**

- Make a list of everything you've been told about yourself that doesn't line up with God's Word.

- Destroy the list in some memorable way. Build a fire and burn it. Tear it into a bazillion pieces and throw it off a bridge. Do something with a grand flourish! Post a picture on social media of you destroying your list. Hashtag it #iamenough #madeformorejourney #PFWMadeforMore

- Commit to making God's voice the loudest voice in your life.

- As He speaks to you this week, write down what He is saying.

**On This Week's Playlist:**

*You Say* by Lauren Daigle, *Who You Say I Am* by Hillsong Worship

# Chapter 3 — You Were Made for More Than Unhealthy Relationships

*Surround yourself with the dreamers and the doers, the believers and thinkers, but most of all, surround yourself with those who see the greatness within you, even when you don't see it yourself.*
*~ Edmund Lee*

Did you know that Carol Burrett and Lucille Ball were close? The two legendary comedians weren't jealous of one another. They cheered one another on, all throughout their careers. The two acted together, with Burnett appearing on four episodes of *The Lucy Show*, and Ball guest starred on four episodes of *The Carol Burnett Show*. Lucy was Carol's mentor. She affectionately called Carol, "Kid." Ball died on April 26, 1989 – Burnett's birthday. She got flowers that day from her friend with the message, "Happy Birthday, Kid."[16] Lucy and Carol were both made better because of their relationship.

Have you ever heard that you need to be careful about who your close friends are because you're the average of the five people you spend the most time with? In his book, *Friend of a Friend: Understanding the Hidden Networks That Can Transform Your Life and Your Career.* David Burkus argues that it's way bigger than the closest five people. He says that you are the average of all of the people who surround you and that this should be a huge concern for all of us.[17] He says, "Your friends really are your future. And the implication is that you don't just need to be more deliberate about who you're spending the most time with. You need to be examining your entire network and its influence on your life."[18]

Maybe you have never found your people. Who are your people? They are those who are going to spur you on to greater things. Those who, like Jesus, accept you as you are but love you too much to let you stay that way. These individuals are the ones who genuinely care about you. Because they love you very much, they want to see growth in your life. They delight in seeing you flourish. They encourage you on to greater things, to fulfill your potential.

Real friends are a part of your progression. Others are an influence on your stagnation and regression.

The power of strong friends changed everything in Caryl's life…

## Caryl Patterson's Story

I was sexually molested as a child. But like many victims, I buried the memories. Nevertheless, the damage remained evident in my actions and feelings. Most of my life I had no idea what was "wrong" with me. I didn't fit in anywhere. I was too dark for white folks, too light for black folks. Too much "book learning" for most people around me, not enough common sense for the rest of the world. I was not pretty enough, but I was too pretty. All I ever heard were voices telling me that I was "not enough" I became a people pleaser in the most extreme measures imaginable.

Even after I forgave everyone involved in that singular incident in my life (teachers who didn't see, my family, the abuser), I still held on to the "not enough" mentality. I remained a people pleaser for years, even after becoming an ordained minister! I never felt comfortable enough to just be myself. The only person with whom I was ever comfortable was the Holy Spirit. I speak to Him as if He is my best friend. So, the day He led me to walk up to Erika Hendricks and ask how I could get involved in the ministry of PF Women, I immediately complied.

This moment changed my life forever. Before I was ever on the team, the kindness and love shown to me by members on the team began the healing process from years of thinking and believing that I was not enough.

These women didn't know me! Yet, two of them sat down at a table and talked with me as if I was someone worthy of attention. I felt welcomed and loved. I cannot describe the feeling of acceptance those moments invoked.

The Holy Spirit used strong women of God - The PF Women Leadership team - to help me to see my own worth. I became comfortable with myself. I never ever felt less than. When the enemy would tell me, "You don't belong," somehow, one of my sisters would step into the gap and encourage me. I never shared my issues with them; I didn't want to make them feel uncomfortable. They were, I believe, led by God to be there for me when I needed them.

Prior to my life with PF Women, I knew that God had called me. Let me be honest, He called me back when I was a child, but I was afraid. I knew that something was "wrong" with me and so I held back. I held back from my calling for years. I would start something (not just ministry), but then stop because that voice in my head said, "You are not worthy." Everything changed when I started listening to God and His people, instead of that voice and the voices of negative people. I heard them, but I stopped listening to them. I stopped holding back; when God said "Go to Bible College," I went. When He said, "Teach in Bible College," I taught. When He said, "Speak at (my church's) Ladies events," I spoke. When

He said, "Go on missions trips," I went. At no point did the enemy or the naysayers stop telling me that I was unworthy. But I chose to go forward, listening to God and the Women of God that He had placed in my life. I made the choice to not back down; to stop at nothing!

I would never say that this was easy. There is a process to recovery, and it can take years to get over listening to the wrong voice in your head. But if you choose to listen to God and to those who love God and serve Him, it will happen. It did for me.[19]

A big part of Caryl's recovery involved finding her people. Making the right friends. Listening to right voices. That is so important. Because right voices lead to right choices.

In his book, *Necessary Endings*, Henry Cloud says, "The good cannot begin until the bad ends."[20]

I'll also go as far to say the great cannot begin until the good ends.

What are you settling for in your life?

Are you settling for friends that sometimes tear you down (even subtly or passive-aggressively) rather than build you up?

Are you settling for relationships that constantly swirl with drama?

Are you settling for friendships that are mostly based on commiserating and negative talk?

Are you settling for a man you have been dating who wants to have sex with you, move in with you but not marry you?

What would it look like for you to let go of these unhealthy relationships and move toward what God has for you?

How long are you going to keep on watering dead plants?

Cloud says:

Your business and your life will change when you really, really get it that some people are not going to change, no matter what you do, and that still others have a vested interest in being destructive. Once you accept that, some very necessary endings get much easier to do. But until then, you might find yourself laboring much longer than you should, still trying to get someone to change, thinking that one more coaching session will do the trick – one more bit of encouragement, or one more session of feedback or confrontation. Or worse, one more concession.[21]

Most of the time, **you already know what you need to do.**

You just haven't had the courage to do it yet.

Friend, let me encourage you that peace is on the other side of that decision.

A new life is possible for you once you have made that choice.

Maybe you have hung onto shallow or toxic relationships because you're not sure if there is a better replacement. Let me save you some research time. The answer is, YES!

There is better for you than shallow.

There is better for you than toxic.

I have often counseled people who are dating the wrong person and advised, "You've got to get rid of Mr. Wrong to make room for Mr. Right." The truth is, if you don't let go, you'll never know what could have been!

You do not need another counseling session.

You don't need to "set out a fleece." (God, if you want me to break up with them, let the light bulb above me shatter, right now...)

You do not need to pray about it any longer.

# 34

You already know.

In your heart of hearts, you know.

Years ago, when I first moved to Tampa, I needed a hairdresser. It was evidently really apparent when one older lady in the church, who was rather brash, walked up to me and said, "Oh dear, what are we going to do with you? You're starting to look like a skunk!" (No, I'm not kidding.) I began to seek out hairdressers, particularly one who was good with color. Tricia[22], a woman in our church, approached me and told me she wanted to be my hairdresser. She worked at Pizzazz[23], a local shop in town, and let me know she had a time slot waiting for me. I hadn't known anything about Tricia prior to this, as we had just been at the church a short time, and this was our first conversation.

My first appointment with Tricia proved to be a wonderful choice where my hairstyle was concerned. Not only did I go with a new, shorter and trendier style, but she was fabulous with color. There was only one problem. I left with a horrible headache. This had nothing to do with the way Tricia styled my hair. The issue was what she would talk about the entire time she was working on me. She was one of the most pessimistic people I ever met, and every question she asked me or statement she made was laced with gossip. Any positive word I would say, she'd turn into a negative. This repeated itself each month. I remember on one occasion I excitedly told her that a newcomer to the church had received Christ the previous month and had been clean ever since from a cocaine addiction. No sooner did I relay this amazing testimony did she cynically retort, "Don't worry, he'll fall. They all do." Each time I left the shop my hair looked great, but my head throbbed, and I felt like I needed to take a shower to wash all the "ick" off me…the ick of negativity, cynicism, sarcasm, doubt, unbelief, gossip and more. But I kept going to Tricia. There were a variety of reasons:

I was afraid if I stopped going to her, there would be ramifications at the church.

I was afraid to have the difficult conversation with her to tell her I wasn't coming anymore.

I was afraid I wouldn't find someone else to do my hair as well.

Afraid, afraid, afraid.

There's a reason the Bible tells us more than 365 times not to be afraid!

I didn't need a "sign" to leave Tricia.

I *knew* I needed to.

The fact was, she was not going to change even if I confronted her. I knew this in my heart.

Leaving was what needed to happen.

Despite me knowing this, fear got the best of me for a while, and I stalled by praying, "God, give me a sign."

A few weeks later, I was getting a nail fill at a shop in Tampa. I didn't know any of the customers who were in the shop that day, and I had come by myself. I sat quietly as the tech did my nails, taking in the sights and sounds around me. Two women were at two other stations behind me, having their nails done. They were obviously friends, sharing conversation during their manicures. This is the conversation I heard:

Friend #1: "Hey, do you still go to Tricia over at Pizzazz?

Friend #2: (Laughing) Oh, heck no! I stopped going to her long ago.

Friend #1: Seriously? Why did you stop?

Friend #2: I had a headache every time I left there. Her negativity drives me crazy. I couldn't take it anymore.

Friend #1: Well, that's exactly why I stopped going last year, I just hadn't mentioned anything to you about it.

I sat there with my mouth hanging open. I got my sign! (As though I needed one!)

By this time, I had made a few more friends in Tampa and I noticed a woman whose cut and color were always stunning. I asked who her stylist was, and she recommended Ada Alfonso. That month, seventeen years ago, Ada Alfonso started doing my hair and has been doing it ever since. My monthly trip to her is one of my favorite times, not only because she's an expert with color, but because my life has changed in many ways because of her. She's a Spirit-filled Christian who exudes love and the wisdom of God. Sitting in her chair each month over the course of almost two decades, I've received prayer, counsel, love and so much more. And the ministry goes both ways! We are mutually edified during our times together. I can't imagine my life (or my hair) without Ada!

If I never had the courage to let go of Tricia, I wouldn't have experienced this 17-year+ blessing of Ada in my life.

You may wonder if any of my fears came true.

Remember...

- I was afraid if I stopped going to Tricia, it would have ramifications of some sort at the church.

Truthfully, there were ramifications. She was offended that I changed hairdressers, and she left the church. I hold no bitterness towards her and pray for her to be blessed. I never talked to others in the church about it at the time, but no one seemed upset over her departure and if they were, they didn't say anything to my husband or me. Perhaps the church members knew she was perpetually offended and not open to changing her ways. I honestly don't know, but the church ended up just fine. It's God's church, not mine and He is in control. God is bigger than any person or problem.

- I was afraid to have the difficult conversation with Tricia to tell her I wasn't coming anymore.

Guess what? I survived the difficult conversation. So did she, although she didn't change.

- I was afraid I wouldn't find someone else to do my hair as well.

I did find someone. She was greater than I ever dreamed.

Remember, the scripture repeatedly cautions us against fear.

John 14:27 says, "Do not let your hearts be troubled, and do not be afraid."

2 Timothy 1:7 says, "For God gave us a spirit not of fear but of power and love and self-control."

Fear will cause you to miss out on countless blessings in your life.

Part of the hindrance to those blessings is the fear of and refusal to make a necessary ending. Make the decision you know is right through the power and strength of God. You don't have to keep wandering around in the realm of toxicity and mediocrity. God has given you the fortitude to make this decision and stick to it!

What are you waiting on, my friend?

Who or what do you need to let go of in order to receive the more than you're made for?

**This Week's Assignments:**

- Make the necessary ending in your life. Do it. Stop stalling.

- Post on social media about what God is showing you. Use the hashtag #PFWMadeforMore

**On This Week's Playlist**:

*I Surrender* by Hillsong, *I Surrender All* by Cece Winans

# Chapter 4 — You Were Made for More Than Secrets

*Nothing makes us so lonely as our secrets.*
*~ Paul Tournier*

A facility made with two-foot thick walls guards it.

There are round-the-clock surveillance, armed guards and unique pin codes for the building.

Only two people can open it, and it must be done with both present.

Is it a bomb? A missile? A huge diamond?

Nope, it's the recipe for KFC fried chicken![24]

To keep the KFC secret even further under wraps, not all the spices are mixed in one place. Half are mixed in one location and then this mixture is taken to another location to be mixed fully so that no one knows all the spices that are present.

Similarly, the recipe for Coca Cola is also such a huge secret that only two executives know the formula and it is fiercely guarded by keeping it under lock and key in the Sun Trust Bank in Atlanta.[25]

A secret like a chicken or beverage recipe is not going to harm anyone. In fact, it is essential in business matters such as these. On the contrary, personal and family secrets can bring so much devastation to people and to families that the ramifications can't even be fully described.

One Sunday morning I was preaching at a church in Ohio, and, as part of the message, I shared a testimony of being reunited with my birth mother and maternal side of the family. Although it was a brief illustration within the message, it seemed to really connect with a few people. One of those people was Claire, an elderly lady who played the organ that morning. During the altar call, Claire left her place on the organ bench, and came forward. With her worn and frail hands clasped in mine she whispered, "I've been a member here and played the organ for over thirty years. I've never told anyone this, but over forty years ago, I gave up a baby girl for adoption. No one in this church knows. I fear them knowing. But this has been an ache in my heart all these years. The pain of loss has never gone away. Will you pray for me?" I did pray for her and then she asked me, "Should I search for her?" I answered that only the Lord could give her an answer and that she should pray and ask Him what she should do, and that I would be praying with her.

After two weeks of prayer, Claire called me. She said, "I was praying, and God told me not to search, but He was clear that I am not to keep this a secret anymore. It has been affecting me all these years, and it's time to get free." I said that I was glad she had heard clearly from God and to keep me informed as to how things were going. During the next month, Claire told everyone her story. She shared it with the women's ministries group at her church. She shared it with her entire family. To her surprise, everyone embraced her and was thankful she shared with them. For the first time, she was not carrying the weight of the heavy secret.

After a month had passed by, Claire was at home one afternoon when the phone rang. The voice on the other end said, "Is this Claire?" When she answered yes, the woman said, "Claire, my name is Susan, and I think you're my mother." You can imagine the shock. When Claire called me, she said, "I marvel at the Lord's working! He knew I needed to hear the sermon that morning and prepare for what was coming. He knew Susan was searching and I didn't need to. He knew I had to open my heart, let out my secret, and prepare not only me, but everyone else for what was coming!"

Nothing will keep you so lonely or hold you in bondage as a secret will.

A study was done with over 2,000 participants regarding secrets and the effects of keeping them. The researchers analyzed the effects of more than 13,000 secrets the participants kept. The research showed that when people keep a secret, they have feelings of inauthenticity that are associated with a lower quality of relationships and lower satisfaction levels with their personal connections.[26]

One of the tenets of many 12-step recovery programs is, "You're only as sick as your secrets."[27] Psychologists say that keeping secrets destroys relationships, affects children's lives, causes suspicion and resentment, creates a false sense of reality and causes illness.[28]

Keeping secrets literally hurts. It is connected to lower well-being, has health ramifications and causes increased anxiety and depression. In time, it causes disease. One of the reasons for this is that it causes so much work to keep a secret. You must watch every word you say. You can't have open conversations, freely talking about just anything. A minor slip-up could spill your secret. Certain topics strike fear in your heart. You avoid various conversations. More than anything, keeping secrets is absolutely exhausting.[29]

45

Secrets keep people in bondage.

What is a bondage?

According to various dictionaries[30] bondage means:

- *The condition of not being free because you are strongly influenced by something or someone.*
- *Slavery or involuntary servitude.*
- *The state of being bound by or subjected to some external power or control.*

One of the things to remember about bondage is that it's simply this:

A **bond** with **age.**

Bondage is something that has kept you bound – tied up – in its grip for a while.

John 5:1-6 tells the story of a man who had been paralyzed for 38 years:

Sometime later, Jesus went up to Jerusalem for one of the Jewish festivals. Now there is in Jerusalem near the Sheep Gate a pool, which in Aramaic is called Bethesda and which is surrounded by five covered colonnades. Here a great number of disabled people used to lie—the blind, the lame, the paralyzed. One who was there had been an invalid for thirty-eight years. When Jesus saw him lying there and learned that he had been in this condition for a long time, he asked him, "Do you want to get well?"[31]

Notice that Jesus asked him if he **wanted** to get well. That's an entire sermon in itself!

Jesus already knows that everyone doesn't want to get well. Some people want to hold on to that which causes them pain. Jesus knew the man would have to *want* his life to change. He would have to *want* to be free.

Let's establish two things before we continue.

1) Some people are in pain, particularly physical pain, and would give anything to not be.

2) A proper theology of suffering is important. Jesus suffered. The disciples suffered. Everyone who has ever been alive has suffered and it is a part of life. You can't escape suffering

I don't deny these truths. What I am saying is this:

**Although suffering is a part of life, secrets cause needless suffering.**

You don't have to continue in secret pain.

Licensed Professional Counselor, Melissa Valerga, goes into more detail about what secrets do to people and to families:

Where there is secrecy, there is shame. Anywhere we find ourselves hiding, then like in the Garden of Eden, we know that we are experiencing and living out of shame. God invites us to come into the light and be healed. He wants to set us free of those things and he knows that what we don't articulate becomes a bondage.

Articulation and putting things into words is so important. He used the word to speak Creation into existence. Jesus is the Word. He gave us His Word. Something about speaking things sets things in motion, in your brain (changing neurological pathways) and in the Spirit. It produces something in our life when we speak. God tells us to confess (speak to another) for two purposes. When we confess to Him, we receive forgiveness (1 John 1:9). When we confess to another, we receive healing (James 5:16). Confession to God alone is not enough. Nor does it bring about the healing He wants us to receive. We need to share our secrets with both Him and others to receive both forgiveness AND healing.

Holding secrets produces, first and foremost, isolation. Shame, which comes from secrets, created a sense of lost relationship with God (again, going back to the

Garden of Eden) and from each other. Families that have secrets will be disconnected in some way, from each other, and from others outside. There will not be true unity. They will not be well. They will simply be covering the sickness, facilitating and nurturing it unintentionally. Once shame (due to secrecy) is present, all sorts of reactions occur. For some, this is rebellion, others this is codependency, others it's addictions, others it's anger, others it's abuse done to others out of inner hurts improperly externalized. The possibilities are endless—chronic grief, insecurities, learned powerlessness, defensiveness, self-reliance, callousness, loneliness, blame, resentment, communication problems, etc.

The damage done by secrets doesn't get better unless the secret is exposed. For some, they need to do this publicly. For others, they choose to do this with a few trusted friends and/or a therapist. How the secret is shared is up to the individual, but exposure is always necessary. Truly, truth sets us, and others, free.

Many times, for those who benefit from or are familiar with the bondage/sickness, there is a backlash against the exposure. The exposure is often blamed as the problem or the person who did the exposing rather than the secret itself. This is because exposure disrupts the dysfunctional system. It is meant to. For dysfunction to change, it must be disrupted. This can be uncomfortable. Exposure presents the opportunity for wellness where there was not. Whole families and systems can be made well. If they are not receptive to a new system of open communication that allows healings, sometimes it is just the individuals themselves who are made well. They no longer carry the weight of the secret and its accompanying shame.

On the other side of exposure comes relief (sometimes immediately and sometimes eventually). And true healing. Thriving. But if the secret is in place, the best we can hope for is coping or surviving.[32]

Do you deal with pain, especially emotional pain, from secrets you know could be addressed and quite possibly healed, but you are resistant to whatever it's going to take to be free?

The enemy will have you convinced that if anyone knew your secret, they would not accept you anymore.

That is a lie.

### Rachel Caruso's Story

I was in bondage for many years to drugs. In 2004 I encountered Christ in a way that changed me forever. When I moved to another county to begin my new life in Christ, I had no shame and no guilt about my former lifestyle of addiction, and I began to share my story with everyone right away. I was so in love with Jesus and I felt so free. I shared about being molested. I shared because I saw that it helped others have hope – especially young people. The only thing I decided I wouldn't share was my abortion. It wasn't talked about in the church, and even though I knew everyone loved me and accepted me, I felt that I shouldn't share it. The reason was because abortion wasn't really talked about and was so looked down upon, I felt I shouldn't share it. I knew that I was forgiven, so I told God that it was our secret.

The Lord had restored my relationship with my children's dad who used to be my drug dealer. He became a believer, we got married, and both of us were living for Christ, sharing a new testimony of a family restored.

Once we were a family and involved in doing family things, I kept thinking about my baby that I had aborted. I knew he was a boy, and I couldn't stop thinking about him. It was hard to enjoy watching my other children in sports. I felt too much time had passed, and because it was my husband's baby and I never told him that I did that, I still thought I would just have to deal with it on my own. I thought, "There's no way I can tell him now…",

In 2007, I was offered a position in full-time ministry. It was at a pregnancy care center. I walked into the office for my interview and was told I could look around. I saw some babies there – with fetal development up to 20 weeks, and when I saw the 12-week-old baby I can't describe it other than feeling like I was being ripped apart on the inside. I was so ignorant about fetal development that even though I had children, I had no idea. Somehow, I finished the interview, and I know it was the Holy Spirit helping me. Once I left and was in the car, I let it out...tears, screaming, angry, hurt and feeling a little betrayed by God. I was talking to Him about it, trying to understand why He didn't prepare me.

I knew that I was going to get that position and I didn't understand what God was doing. They were pro-life, and I had murdered my baby. After two weeks of complete emotional craziness, I finally told my boss. She was very understanding, walked me through it, and I was able to go through post-abortion healing. I told my husband and he, too, was very forgiving. I also told my children and they forgave me as well.

The Lord opened the door for me to share my story with over 1,000 people. Just prior to that, we were also able to have a small memorial for my son Issachar. I had named him Daniel but when I went through post-abortion healing, I asked God what his name was because He had him before I ever even acknowledged him. He gave me the name Issachar, which means, "will be a great reward." I thought I heard him wrong until one of my girls I was going through the post-abortion healing class with helped me to understand that many babies' lives were being saved already through him.

Fast forward to my first grandchild being born...my son and his wife asked if they could name him after Issachar. I could not believe it! Again, God gave me a little "face of grace." I could hear Him saying, "Rachel, you are never allowed to have shame or guilt regarding Issachar, because every time I look at his little face or think of him all I have is joy!" I ended up working in that ministry for three years and then I was the given the opportunity to be director at their drug rehab and now I have come back to full circle, working with the same pregnancy care center again. I feel like Issachar's reward is to defend life here on earth until I see Jesus face to face

I share with women that the deepest darkest thing you have done in your life will be the thing that God will use the most, if you confess it. You will find freedom, and you will help others find freedom.[33]

There are various ways to free ourselves of unnecessary pain. Some of those ways are:

**Confession & Prayer:** James 5:16 (NIV) says, "Therefore confess your sins to each other and pray for each other so that you may be healed. The prayer of a righteous person is powerful and effective."

**Counseling:** Proverbs 15:22 (NIV) "Without consultation, plans are frustrated, but with many counselors they succeed." And Proverbs 24:6 (NIV) "...in abundance of counselors there is victory."

**Worship:** 2 Corinthians 3:17-18 (NIV) "Now the Lord is the Spirit, and where the Spirit of the Lord is, there is freedom. And we, who with unveiled faces all reflect the glory of the Lord, are being transformed into His image with intensifying glory, which comes from the Lord, who is the Spirit."

**Meditating on God's Word**: 1 Timothy 4:15 (NIV) "Practice these things, immerse yourself in them, so that all may see your progress." Romans 8:6 (NIV) "The mind governed by the flesh is death, but the mind governed by the Spirit is life and peace."

**Sharing our story:** Revelation 12:11 (NIV) "They triumphed over him [Satan] by the blood of the Lamb and by the word of their testimony."

The worst thing we can do is hide the secret and suppress our feelings. It affects our relationship with God, and with others. Sorge says: "Jesus can handle the confession of our actual struggles; what He can't handle is when we hide them and pretend they don't exist. The secret place is no place for secrets. It's the place for total honesty and full disclosure. When we reveal our struggles, He releases the grace to help us change."[34]

Have you ever heard the adage, "Time heals all wounds?"

It's a lie.

Only Jesus, plus time, can heal a wound.

When I was a little girl, my mother was cooking chicken noodle soup on the stove – one of my favorite lunches. I was so young, I don't remember anything before the incident that day, other than the pot of boiling soup coming down on me from the stove and my screams which led to being rushed to the emergency room. My mother had turned from the stove for a moment, an innocent mistake any mom could make, and my little fingers brought the pot down on me, burning me with first, second, and third degree burns on the front of my body. My only memory afterwards is of the screaming while I was being laid down on the sofa, my clothes taken off and then being taken to the hospital. After that, my memory of being back at our house is of being wrapped for several weeks, and the pain that happened each time those bandages had to be taken off, redressed and rewrapped. It was excruciating. A few weeks after the burn, the doctor said my bandages had to come off and my skin needed to be exposed to the air so it would heal. I can remember screaming that I didn't want them to take the bandages off. But they had to be taken off for me to progress. My parents and church family prayed for me that God would heal me quickly and I would not have any scars. And, praise God, I have no scars. As my mother says of this incident, "God truly is a God of miracles!"

Anything you cover forever doesn't heal well. Wounds may be kept under wraps for a short time but in due course they need to be aired in order to experience proper healing.

What are you covering that would heal if only you would step forward into the light of God's love and the love of His people?

I can almost guarantee they will embrace you. If they don't, guess what? They're not your people.

You were made for more than living a secret life.

You were made for more than hiding.

It's time to be free of your secret.

**This Week's Assignments:**

- Make a list of anything you are in bondage to.

- Make a list of ways you are going to address that bondage. (i.e. confession, prayer, counsel)

- Find at least one strong Christian woman that you can share with this week about this. If you are carrying a secret, confess it.

- If you don't carry any painful secrets, pray that God will keep you from it, and use you to help others to find freedom.

- Post on social media about what God is showing you. Use the hashtag #PFWMadeforMore and #Nomoresecrets

**On This Week's Playlist:**

*Holy Water* by We the Kingdom, *Unspoken* by Open the Clouds, *Graves into Gardens* by Elevation Worship, *Stand in Your Love* by Cory Asbury and Brandon Lake

# Chapter 5 — You Were Made for More Than Shrinking

*Be yourself. Everyone else is already taken.*
*~ Oscar Wilde*

**WARNING**

Not everything I share in this chapter will make you want to do cartwheels.

In fact, it may depress the daylights out of you for a few minutes. But hold on...

You need this.

Get a cup of coffee, round up a Hershey Kiss, take two Tylenols. Do whatever you need to do to be able to allow me to say some hard things here. Because every woman needs to hear it.

Women have been told to be quiet for foreeeeeeeever.

In 800 B.C. Homer wrote a poem called *The Odyssey*. In this poem, Odysseus' son Telemachus tells his mother,

Penelope, "Go back up into your quarters. Speech will be the business of men."[35]

In 100 A.D. Greek orator Dio Chrystostom asks his audience, "If men's voices all suddenly turned female, would not that seem terrible and harder to bear than any plague?"[36]

In 1907 Henry James warned that American women will turn the English language into a "generalized mumble or jumble, a tongueless slobber or snarl or whine," like "the moo of a cow, the bray of the ass, and the bark of the dog."[37]

In 1924, an associate at Westinghouse Broadcasting told a reporter he would never let a woman hold forth on the air: "Their voices are flat or they are shrill, and they are usually pitched far too high to be modulated correctly."[38]

In 2001, Apple introduced Siri. Microsoft followed with Cortana, and Amazon with Alexa. "Female voices are seen, on average, as less intelligent than male voices," notes Clifford Nass, an authority on computer-human interactions. But for traditionally gendered tasks such as secretarial duties, "female voices are easier to hear."[39]

And it's still happening today. This same archaic mumbo jumbo continues.

(Go get the Hershey Kiss if you haven't already. And a strong coffee. I'll wait.)

Welcome back.

Miriam[40] is a middle aged, single Christian woman who has a corporate job and professionally models as a side job. She is very well known in the community as a philanthropist who leads many worthy projects. Miriam graduated in the top of her high school and college classes and is a brilliant conversationalist. She makes good money. Although Miriam is single, she has always wanted to get married but doesn't get asked out on many dates. One day her pastor approached her unsolicited, and said, "Miriam, I just want to speak into your life and tell you that marriage would probably happen much easier for you if you changed your personality to not be so outgoing. A quiet demeanor would suit you better, and men wouldn't be so intimidated by you."

Although Miriam has a deep desire to be a wife, she is not willing to leave her God-given personality behind to do so. Maybe you're thinking, "Well, is she abrasive? Is she threatening?" No, and no. She presents herself with incredible grace and kindness on and off the stage. The truth is many people are intimidated by her because she's the total package. She's gorgeous, she's smart, she's talented and she is fearless. She also makes good money and she's not desperate.

It's a fact that many people are intimidated by intelligent people.

It's a fact that many people are threatened by talented people.

It's a fact that many people are uncomfortable with a person who is a strong and assertive communicator.

It's a fact that when you are woman, this problem can be worse.

(Go ahead, get another Hershey Kiss.)

Many women respond to this problem by doing just as Miriam's pastor advised her to do. They morph into whatever and whoever they need to be to get what they long for.

Treena[41] is a young lady who was engaged to a pastor. She was called to the ministry during a youth camp. When she graduated high school, she headed to Bible college, graduated with a ministry degree and became a credentialed minister. Midway through the engagement, her fiancée, Josh[42] asked if she loved him enough to give up her credentials. He was uncomfortable with her having ministerial credentials of her own. He felt it was important that it be clear to the church that he was the one in the ministry and she was his supporter. Reluctantly, Treena gave up her ministerial license because she didn't want to lose Josh. Her pastor had counseled her that she would come to regret this, but she couldn't bear to lose Josh, which is what would take place if she kept her credentials.

Any woman who has shrunk herself down to please anyone other than God can testify that t leads to a horrible ache in your soul. To walk away from who God has made you to be creates a gnawing sense inside you for life where you know you aren't living out His design and destiny for you.

In the Bible, in John 3:30, John, referring to Jesus said, "He must increase, I must decrease."

We need to put Jesus in His rightful place in our lives – Savior and Lord. He is exalted above all else, and in everything we do, He must become greater, we must become less.

**Jesus is the only person you should be shrinking yourself down for.**

**Jesus is the ONLY ONE who has the authority to ask you to become smaller.**

That doesn't mean you become prideful.

It doesn't mean you have a lack of humility.

It doesn't mean you become selfish.

It doesn't mean you think you are better than others.

What this is about is being willing to live out who God has called you to be, and to utilize all the gifts He has given you.

It's about living your divine design – nothing more, nothing less, nothing else.

Are you a strong communicator? Communicate with confidence.

Are you a minister? Do not be afraid to say, "I am a minister."

Are you a writer? Do you write blog posts and articles? Do you have a desire to write a book or have you written a book? Stop avoiding saying it outright when people ask you. Don't say, "I dabble with writing sometimes."

Say it out loud right now: "I am a writer."

Say it again stronger: "I am a writer."

STOP looking for someone to marry to "go into the ministry."

You go into the ministry by going into the ministry.

Do you possess the qualifications to lead your department at work, and the position is open? Apply for it. Stop talking yourself out of it.

Are you a high school girl who is good at math? Are you on the honor roll? Own it. Stop hiding. Stop pretending you're dumb just to fit in. You're not dumb, and fitting in is overrated. Most world changers don't fit in.

Has God called you to be a missionary? Are you single? Stop waiting to meet a man who will "lead you to the field." Jesus is leading you to the field. The Great Commission is for all people! Go!

You will never be content making yourself smaller for people who can't handle you. If they can't handle you, they aren't your people.

You will never find joy in downplaying and dismissing your abilities to make other people more comfortable around you.

You will never be fulfilled fitting into someone else's mold to fit their expectations. A friend of mine often says, "When you fit into someone else's mold, you just become moldy."

If your friends seem unsettled by your capabilities, get yourself a group of new friends. Stop reducing yourself to fit people you have outgrown. Your circle needs to be cheering for you the loudest. If they aren't – find a new circle.

"But I'm going to be lonely," you say.

"I might not ever get married," you say.

"Everybody might hate me," you say.

"I might not ever have a best friend," you say.

If you shrink yourself down to fit other people's desires, you're just trading one misery for another. You're getting a one-way ticket to hating your future life.

(Go ahead. Get two Hershey Kisses.)

The way many women are raised is a contributor to the challenge of feeling as if they need to shrink to make it in the world. Many of us were taught to keep quiet about our talents, with the instruction that, in due time, God would reveal to others what we have to offer. We have been trained that it is wrong to receive credit for what we accomplish. Not only have we been taught that it's wrong to celebrate wins, but we are admonished that other people probably won't like us if we do. Boys, on the other hand, are encouraged to come out swinging and compete from the time they exit the womb. They are urged to play to win, and even to crush others on the field, whether it be the football field, a military mission or in competition for a job. They are lauded for their accomplishments in the world and in the church. Meanwhile, girls are instructed to be okay with quietly serving behind the scenes in hopes that someone will notice us. To clarify, most Christian women are not looking to crush anyone, we just want a seat at the table.

You've heard 3,682 messages about quietly and patiently waiting for your Boaz.

(Sigh)

This. Has. To. Stop.

And one of the only ways it will stop is if we refuse to play along.

When we refuse to be silent.

When we refuse to be someone we are not.

When we refuse to wait for permission to be who God created us to be.

It will happen when we as a sisterhood decide that collectively, we are DONE with small living. D.L. Moody once said, "If God is your partner, make your plans big!"

This isn't about becoming a braggart. That's not attractive on a man or a woman. This is about stepping up to live out your God-given design.

**Judi Cotignola's Story**

I grew up in a fourth generation Assemblies of God minister's home. My great-great grandmother, Lula Mae Doggett, had credentials with the Assemblies of God before she married. She was an itinerant preacher throughout all of Oklahoma and Kansas. This was the model that I most closely identified with, but this was not the model that I saw played out in my everyday life. The boys in the family were automatically given a position, a platform, and opportunities to preach and teach. I was asked to work with children. Not that working with kids is not a calling – it just wasn't mine.

I wandered from the church for a while. I stayed connected to God but didn't feel like what was offered to me as ministry was what God was calling me to do. I didn't know how to articulate what He was leading me to do.

Seventeen years ago, we came back to Florida and started serving at the church where my Dad was senior pastor. A year later my husband left his secular job and came on staff at the church. I still felt like God specifically called me to ministry in a different way than I had seen modeled by women in our family, but I didn't know how to express it. I received a package in the mail from a ministry called Pastoring Partners, and I knew in my heart that this was what I had been searching for. These were women who weren't just called alongside to be an encourager, but they were called as equals with their husband. They were full co-laborers in Christ. I felt like God was asking me to get credentials, not to justify my calling but to hone my craft. I graduated from an AG Bible college, but my degree was in communications. I wanted greater ministerial training to prepare for the future.

My father was one who recognized the calling and anointing upon my life. It was he who invited me to begin preaching at the church. When some female members of the family found out that I was enrolling in the district school of ministry, they asked me why. I explained that God had called me to preach and teach. They asked me if I was trying to take over my husband's job. The answer was no. As people in the church began referring to me as Pastor Judi, these same family members asked me why. Why couldn't I just be "Judi" as I had always been? Why did I need to be referred to as a pastor? I was asked how what I was doing was any different from what the other women in our family have done longer than I had been alive. The short answer was — I preached every Sunday night. I led multiple Bible studies throughout the week. I led staff meetings and staff members. I spoke occasionally on Sunday mornings.

The women in my family were strong leaders who had helped their husbands with anything needed, but they didn't identify as ministers. I felt God was calling me to specifically preach and teach. I sensed that I was to own the calling God placed on my life and not dumb it down because it made other people around me uncomfortable.

I am now a licensed minister and I will be ordained in May of 2021 with the Assemblies of God. Since stepping out into the fullness of my call, God has opened doors and it so happens that now I am the one who is invited to preach more than my husband. He is not threatened or intimidated and supports me in that in every way. I feel strongly that I need to own this call not only for me, but for my three daughters who are each called as well. The only regret I have is not starting sooner. I encourage every woman out there who is called to own it now. Find other people who are walking the same path. Get a mentor. Find people who have been down the road longer than you to speak into your life. It's not too late to be who and what God has called you to be.[43]

**WARNING**

The people who will give you the most trouble with you refusing to shrink are those who haven't had the courage to stop shrinking themselves!! Their envy of you often turns into disdain for you. They will be angry that you had the courage to go through the trials you did to get where you are now while they remained unwilling to pay the price.

It's sad but you can't let that get to you. Let them talk. Let them try to block you from opportunities and influence. Don't worry about that. Leave it to God. What He has for you is for you! God will open a door that nobody can shut! Your times and your future are in His hands. And so is justice. As one of my heroes, Evangelist Martha Tennison, says, "God keeps good books, and payday's not always on Friday!"

Don't dwell on what they are doing. Don't harmonize with whatever they are saying. Keep your focus.

What is your focus? It's what God is telling you. It's what He's asking you to do. Sometimes you must keep the proverbial blinders on to get to the "more" that God has for you. All that matters is what He says.

Ralph Waldo Emerson once said, "To be yourself in a world that is constantly trying to make you something else is the greatest accomplishment."

Within Christianity scriptures are twisted to justify this malarkey. It can be overwhelming at times, but I've come to see this challenge from a hope-filled place. And it's only through the power of God. I believe that despite the world being this way, nothing is impossible with God. It's a fact that this is a problem in the world and the church. But God's truth is more important than facts. If God fashioned you to be a certain way, and He gave you a unique skill set, He's able to cut through the injustice that is still present in our culture to make you what you're intended to be, and get you where you need to be without becoming someone and something you're not.

Jeremiah 17:7 (NLT) says, "But blessed are those who trust in the Lord and have made the Lord their hope and confidence." Our confidence is not to be in any man-made political systems in the world or in the church. Our hope is not to be in what has been promised to us by people. Our hope must be in the Lord!

Philippians 1:6 (NLT) says: "And I am certain that God, who began the good work within you, will continue his work until it is finally finished on the day when Christ Jesus returns." He has begun a good work in you. He will finish it. You must cooperate. Do not shrink. Refuse to turn back! Work with Him and what He has given you!

Whose voice is louder in your life? The voice of God or the voices of the people who try to diminish you? Who are you submitted to? God or the voices of the people? Galatians 1:10 says, "Am I now trying to win the approval of human beings, or of God? Or am I trying to please people? If I were still trying to please people, I would not be a servant of Christ."

Many people mention a desire for God to be on their side. Let me let you in on a secret I've always lived by. I don't pray for God to be on my side. The key is to always be on **His** side. If I'm always on His side, I never have to worry about winning.

**God always wins. When you make sure you're on His side, you're always going to win.**

When God says get up, get up!

When God says go, go!

When God says speak, speak!

In his book, *Forgotten God*, author Francis Chan says, "I want to live so that I am truly submitted to the Spirit's leading on a daily basis. Christ said it is better for us that the Spirit came, and I want to live like I know that is true. I don't want to keep crawling when I have the ability to fly."

Fly, sister, fly. I don't care if they're screaming at you to crawl. FLY!

**This Week's Assignments:**

- Make a list of any ways you have been shrinking or holding back from who God has called you to be and what He has called you to be. (The first step to moving forward is to define reality.)

- One you have made the list, go sit in front of a mirror. Name each thing on your list and say out loud: "I am no longer going to shrink back from_____. For instance, if you're hiding the fact that you are called to lead, look at yourself in the mirror and say, "I am no longer going to shrink back from leading. I am called to lead." Say this with each item on the list. Say it louder! Say it in the mirror until you believe it!

- Hold the list in your hands after you make these declarations. Go through each item and pray over it. Ask the Lord to give you strength to stop shrinking down. Ask Him to specifically show you how to stand stronger in who He has called you to be.

- Journal this week about what God is saying to you about your design and destiny.

- Get a bag of Hershey Kisses. Give some out to girls and women this week who surround you and tell them they are made for more.

- Post online what God is showing you this week. Use the hashtag #notshrinking #PFWMadeformore

**On This Week's Playlist:**

*Confidence* by Santus Real, *Yes and Amen* by Chris Tomlin, *Goodness of God* by Jenn Johnson, *Oceans (Where Feet May Fail)* by Hillsong United

# Chapter 6 — You Were Made for More than Exhaustion

*A being is free only when it can determine and limit its activity.*
*~ Karl Barth*

What do all these things have in common?[44]

- The Exxon Valdez Oil Spill
- The Three Mile Island Accident
- The Challenger Explosion
- The Air France Flight 447 crash
- The Great Neck High-Speed Train Crash
- The American Airlines Flight 1420 Crash
- The Chernobyl Disaster

Every one of these tragedies was caused by exhaustion and sleep deprivation. Sadly, most adults tend to live hurried lives, with little rest. In many cases, it takes a personal tragedy for them to slow down. This is counter to how God created us. The Bible says that He created Sabbath not for Him, but for us! (Mark 2:27) In fact, it was one of the first things He did in Scripture, as a part of creation.

What is a Sabbath? Growing up I thought it was Sunday. I believed it was about honoring the Lord's day and going to church. I'm embarrassed to say that I didn't really know what the Sabbath was until I was in my fifties! Most of what I learned came from my professor and friend, Dr. Chris Corbett. In turn, I have taught those principles that I have learned to those I lead. From Dr. Chris, I learned that taking a weekly Sabbath is twenty-four hours of rest. It is resting, enjoying, delighting in the Lord and those we love. It is doing things that restore, renew and recharge us.

**Amy McNatt's Story**

My husband and I both work in full-time ministry. In the past, we did not get very much rest. We worked seven days a week. We had a "day off" but very rarely took it. Something always came up, someone always needed help, or something needed to be set up at church. I love my job and I love our congregation, but the bottom line is, I was not being obedient to God's word.

I went away to the PF Women Leadership Team Retreat and what do you think the theme of the weekend was? Rest! Deanna Shrodes opened her first message to us by saying, "What if I told you I committed adultery? What about murder? What would you ladies think if I shared with you that I murdered someone?" Everyone in the room just stared in shock. Then Deanna said, "What if I told you I did not take a Sabbath this week? You'd probably think it was no big deal. But the truth is...all three of these sins are included in the Ten Commandments."

As I sat there listening, the Lord started speaking to me and I started making excuses for my behaviors. But graciously and lovingly the Lord kept talking and I started listening. I returned that weekend and began telling my husband about what the Lord had spoken to my heart about a "day of rest". His reply was astonishing to me. He had been talking to his mentor that weekend also and they had been talking about taking a day of rest and how important that was. We started immediately. God got our attention and we were obedient. Our lives have changed. We are not exhausted and worn out all the time like we had been. I have energy and a lot more love to give others. Thank you, God for loving me enough to correct me when I am not being obedient to your word. You are always faithful, loving, merciful and true.[45]

As we approach scripture one of the main problems that we often try to do, unconsciously, is to see Jesus and the Bible through our cultural lens. We see American Jesus. Africans see African Jesus. The Chinese see Chinese Jesus. But Jesus was not American or African or Chinese...He was/is a Jew and the Bible is set in Jewish culture. And so, the more we get to know Jesus, the more we dig into the truths of the Bible through that lens. Keep that in mind as we go forward...

When I am cooking chicken, my bulldog, Manny, immediately runs into the kitchen from wherever he is. Unless he were literally dying, I am certain that Manny would jump for any piece of chicken that might fall from the pan, or that I might drop to him. Nothing will restrain him from going after that chicken. Generally, animals do not think of restraint when it comes to these things, they just do them. On the contrary, men and women are capable of restraint.

When we look back at the story of Adam and Eve in the Garden, one of the things the serpent wanted Eve to do is give in to temptation and eat the apple. He pressed her to show no restraint and take whatever she wanted. His message was, "Did God *really* say you couldn't have that? Why in the world would He not want you to have it? You should go for it and take what you desire." In behaving this way, Eve would be no different from the animals who just go for what they see and want.

One of the names for God is "El Shaddai." It is one of the names for God that is more difficult to translate. The ancient Jewish rabbis said that the name literally should translate "the God that knows when to say enough."[46] God created man and woman and then stopped and said, 'It is very good." He knew man and woman were enough. He knew when to say, "enough." And when He stopped and rested, it was not because He was tired. It was because He knew it was time to be done. Because it wasn't simply good, but *very* good. Because it was enough.

Imagine if a sculptor kept chipping away at a statue as they were making it, without stopping. Imagine if they went on endlessly. It would be horrible and ugly, and amount to nothing but rubble. Imagine if a songwriter never stopped writing a song. It would never be finished and released. It would never bless the world.

God knows when to say "enough." We are made in His image. We are not animals. God has given us the capacity to say, "enough."[47]

Psalm 46:1- says, "Be still and know that I am God." The New American Standard version of the Bible says, "Cease striving and know that I am God."

God wants us to cease striving.

To breathe.

I said that we need to look at scripture and Jesus through a Jewish lens.

Think about this...what time does the day officially start?

Six times, the opening chapter of the Bible says, "And there was evening and there was morning," to signal the completion of a divine day's work. For Jewish people, the day does not begin with the crack of dawn, but rather with the setting of the sun. It is Jewish practice that days are from sunset to sunset.

Technically our day – everyone's day – begins at 12:00 AM. A new day starts at midnight.

Our day officially begins with REST. And it ends as well with REST.

Rest is so important, God structured things so that when a new day begins, we are resting. And when the day ends, we are resting.

Sabbath does not always mean being alone, but to be spiritually healthy we need regular times of solitude. When I'm struggling with questions; quiet time brings the answers. When I want a download from God's heart to mine, it requires solitude. When I want the creativity of the Holy Spirit to flow through me, it takes getting still. When it comes to all the Christian "greats" – from theologians to missionaries and evangelists and other well- known people, I am reminded that there is no difference between them and us, other than a willingness to be consistently in God's presence. That is where all the spiritual meat they feed others comes from. Every world changing idea started in silence. I have learned, the quieter I get, the more I change my world. I may not have changed *the* world yet, but I know I have changed *my* world...my sphere of influence. And it hasn't ever come out of a place of noise.

We often see silence and solitude as unproductive. Yet, it's one of the most productive things you can do. Ultimately, rest makes space in our souls and lives.

Many people mistakenly believe they are leaving a legacy by working as hard as they do. Think again. My grown sons and daughter take more time off than I ever did. They enjoy days off, travel, and fun. I look around me at other young adults and they also don't seem enamored by people who do nothing but work. They don't look up to the people who burn the candle at both ends. They do not look to people as mentors who say they haven't had a day off in years.

"Work-life balance" is a huge thing today in the workplace especially among the younger generation. If we want to leave a legacy, today's generation is not starstruck by leaders who run themselves into the ground and burn out. They do not look up to people who live these types of chaotic lives – who do not have healthy patterns in life. Previous generations honored those who never took a day off. Today's generation does not.

**Deanna's Journal Entry – February 6, 2020**

God, I see people doing things for you, and yet some of them are so unhappy. I don't want to be that way. I can see where I have been this way in the past when I felt forced to do things. How I wish I had people in my life at the time who had the capacity to help me! Ministry doesn't kill people. It's the way they do ministry that kills them! I wish I knew at 20 what I know at 53. Hopefully, I can help people who are beginning. I sit here right now writing in this journal while waves crash on the shore. I realize, they will continue to do so tomorrow. The sun will rise, the sun will set. Birds will fly around. All this is going to go on…it's going to happen whether I am here or not. Life will go on with or without me. So why not let go of my cares and give them to you? Why not rest and take care of myself, so maybe I will be able to see more sunrises and sunsets? I am learning more and more of how body, soul and spirit are connected. All these things need to be fed and cared for, so I can flourish.

After taking two of Dr. Chris's classes where we studied the Sabbath, I became deliberate about it. I went through my calendar for the entire year, carving out a weekly Sabbath. Because of my travel and speaking schedule, my Sabbath often happens on different days of the week within a 7-day period. But I make sure that within each week, there is a Sabbath.

Scheduling out your Sabbaths is something that you must be intentional about. It will never just happen on its own. You'll have to fight for it. It's imperative that you do because it's impossible to fulfill God's will for your life without proper rest.

Fighting for it is worth it. If you do not fight, you will eventually have your own Chernobyl. God has made you for more than exhaustion.

**This Week's Assignments:**

- Start mapping out your Sabbath days for the rest of the year. One day a week – 24 hours of rest each week.

- Stop making excuses. Do this.

- Start with at least five minutes each day that you are alone – completely quiet – and listening for God to speak.

- When God speaks, write down what He says.

- Post online about what God is speaking to you this week about rest. Use the hashtags #noexhaustion #Sabbath #PFWMadeformore

**On This Week's Playlist:**

*Be Still My Soul* and *Here* by Kari Jobe, *Be Still* by Hillsong,

\* \* \*

**A Prayer for You**

Father, I have so enjoyed walking this path of sharing what you have placed in my heart with *Made for More*. Thank you for entrusting me with this book. I am grateful for the help You gave me in redeeming the time and utilizing the opportunity of the Covid-19 shutdown to accomplish your purposes.

I pray that you would help the woman who just read this book to not see it as just another book, but a journey to a new path of the more you have for her.

May she know that she was made for more than rules. Let her realize deep down that she is unconditionally loved by You, and nothing can ever separate her from that love.

May she know that she was made for more than toxic thoughts. Help her to keep her mind focused on You.

May she know that she was made for more than unhealthy relationships. Guide her to her people, Lord. Lead her to her tribe!

May she know that she was made for more than secrets. Set her free!

May she know that she was made for more than shrinking. Help her to live out Your design for her. Strengthen her as she confidently steps out into the more that you have for her.

May she know that she was made for more than exhaustion. Give her rest – real rest. Grant her wisdom and strength in carving out a Sabbath for herself on a weekly basis.

Bless her life, Lord. Bless her like crazy.

In Jesus name,

Amen

## Want More from Deanna?

All of Deanna's books are available in paperback or as an ebook, at Amazon.com.

For more information, go to deannashrodes.net.

# Acknowledgements

Thank you to...

The women of the Peninsular Florida District of the Assemblies of God – Rachel Caruso, Pamela Clayton, Judi Cotignola, Amy McNatt, Caryl Patterson, Marisela Santiago and Dianna Walston, who were willing to share their stories for this book. You are all such courageous women of God.

The PF Women Leadership Team for encouraging me with this project and praying over it. You are simply the best.

Gayle Lechner for doing a masterful job of editing on very quick notice, and just being wonderful you! And for never giving up!

Linda Klippenstein, my pastor and friend, for all the ways you support me as we both follow God's leading into the "more" He has for us. Doing life with you is the best!

Laura Dennis for being willing to turn this around on a dime, edit and publish it. And, for being the greatest friend a gal ever had.

Judi Cotignola for your unwavering support and friendship.

Terry Raburn, my boss, leader, and friend – for always being such an encourager.

My beloved husband Larry, for setting me free to fly.

I cherish you all.

# About the Author

Deanna Doss Shrodes is the Women's Ministries Director for the Pen-Florida District of the Assemblies of God. She is most passionate about investing in leaders and leadership health.

Deanna is an Assemblies of God ordained minister. She is a speaker in demand in the United States and abroad, and is an accomplished musician, worship leader and recording artist. She is an award-winning writer and sole author of five books and contributing writer of five books. Deanna has been featured in many publications worldwide, including The Huffington Post. Deanna holds a Masters in Ministerial Leadership from Southeastern University, and is currently in the doctoral program, also at Southeastern.

Deanna has been married to her college sweetheart, Larry, for 33 years. They have pastored in the Assemblies of God for as long as they have been married and Larry is currently lead pastor of Celebration Church Tampa and presbyter of the Tampa Bay area. Deanna and Larry have three grown children, one grandchild and four nieces and nephews who are the light of their lives. They also have a sweet bulldog named Manchester.

On her day off, Deanna enjoys reading, writing, taking walks, riding her bike and shopping at thrift stores. You can follow Deanna's podcast, the Stronger Leadership Podcast, on your iPhone, Android, or at pfwomen.com.

# References

[1] Kara Ladd, *50 of the Craziest State Laws*, Good Housekeeping, December 2015.
[2] Ibid.
[3] Ibid.
[4] Bob Sorge, *Secrets of the Secret Place*, Oasis House Publishing, 2001, 87.
[5] Marisela Santiago is the Women's Ministries Representative for the Daytona Area of the Pen Florida District of the Assemblies of God. She is also a Regional Leader for PF Women.
[6] Rachel Hodin, *35 Famous People Who Were Painfully Rejected Before Making It Big,* Thought Catalog, October 4, 2013.
[7] Ibid
[8] Ibid
[9] Julie Ma, *25 Famous Women on Overcoming Rejection,* The Cut, September 29, 2016.
[10] Joshua Moraes, *20 Famous People Who Faced Rejection Before They Made It Big*, SW, June 23, 2015.
[11] Ibid
[12] John Maxwell, *How Successful People Think,* Center Street Publishing, 2009.
[13] Caroline Leaf, *How to NOT Let Toxic People, Words or Situations Affect Your Mental Health*, drleaf.com, July 31, 2019.
[14] Pamela Clayton is the Women's Ministries Representative for the Gainesville area of the Pen Florida District of the Assemblies of God, and also serves with PF Women as a regional leader.
[15] Mark Batterson, *Whisper: How to Hear the Voice of God,* Multnomah, 2017, page 11.
[16] Meredith Danko, *12 Lesser Known Historical Friendships*, MF, February 25, 2016
[17] David Burkus, *You're NOT The Average Of The Five People You*

*Surround Yourself With,* Mission.org; May 23, 2018
[18] Ibid.
[19] Caryl Patterson is the Women's Ministries Representative for the Orlando area of the Pen Florida District of the Assemblies of God and also serves as the coordinator of their 1000 Sisters Ministry.
[20] Henry Cloud, *Necessary Endings*, Harper Collins, 2010, 1.
[21] Ibid.
[22] Not her real name
[23] Not the real name of the shop
[24] Vinay Devnath, *15 Of The Most Awesomely Guarded Secrets In The World*, Storypick, February 2016.
[25] Ibid.
[26] Ruben Castaneda, *How Your Secrets Can Damage and Maybe Even Kill You,* U.S. News and World Report, June 26, 2017.
[27] Ibid.
[28] Suzanne Handler, *5 Reasons Why Keeping Family Secrets Could Be Harmful*, Psych Central, July 8, 2018.
[29] Michael Slepien, *Why the Secrets You Keep Are Hurting You*, Scientific American, February 5, 2019.
[30] Dictionary.com, Merriam-Webster, Collins Dictionaries
[31] John 5:1-6 (NIV)
[32] Melissa Valerga is a licensed professional counselor and associate pastor, residing in Edmund, Oklahoma.
[33] Rachel Caruso is the Assistant Director of the Pregnancy & Family Care Center at the Christian Care Center in Leesburg, Florida.
[34] Bob Sorge, Secrets of the Secret Place, Oasis Publishing, 2001; 142.
[35] Julia B. Chan, Maddie Oatman*, A Brief History of Telling Women to Shut Up*, Questia Trusted Online Research
[36] Ibid.
[37] Ibid.
[38] Julia B. Chan and Maddie Oatman, *Men have Been Telling Women to Shut up for at Least 3,000 Years,* Mother Jones, November/December 2018.
[39] Ibid.
[40] Not her real name
[41] Not her real name

[42] Not his real name
[43] Judi Cotignola is a licensed minister with the Assemblies of God and serves as the assistant to the director of PF Women. She is a speaker in demand and leader and mentor to many.
[44] Melynda Sorrels, *10 Truly Devastating Disasters Caused By Sleep Deprivation*, Listverse, November 2018.
[45] Amy McNatt is the Women's Ministries Representative for the Clearwater/St. Peterburg area of the Pen Florida District of the Assemblies of God and also pastors Seminole Assembly of God with her husband, Kenny.
[46] Marty Solomon, the BEMA Podcast, Season 1, Episode 1
[47] Marty Solomon, the BEMA Podcast, Season 1, Episode 1

Made in the USA
Columbia, SC
17 June 2020